PAPER MODELS THAT ROCK!

SIX PENDULUM AUTOMATA

ROB IVES

DOVER PUBLICATIONS, INC.
Mineola, New York

Bibliographical Note

Paper Models That Rock! Six Pendulum Automata is a new work, first published
by Dover Publications, Inc., in 2013.

International Standard Book Number
ISBN-13: 978-0-486-49944-4
ISBN-10: 0-486-49944-8

Manufactured in the United States by Courier Corporation
49944801   2013
www.doverpublications.com

Contents

Introductory Note

The projects in this book are for you to cut out and assemble. Solid black lines are the cut lines. Dotted lines are valley folds, dashed lines are mountain folds. The gray areas indicate where to glue. The gray areas are only marked on the front side of the model sheets. You will need a small selection of common tools: scissors, a craft knife, a ruler, a cutting mat, and glue. A glue spreader is also useful though a coffee stirrer or popsicle stick will also work well for this job.

Before you start cutting, review the project. Take some time to read through all the instructions and look at the photographs. When you are ready, remove the pages from the book.

Using the point of your scissors and ruler, carefully score along the dotted and dashed lines. These lines mark the folds in the model and scoring will help make these folds crisp and accurate. Once you have scored all the dotted and dashed lines use your craft knife to cut out any holes or small areas in the model pieces. Make sure an adult is present while you are using your craft knife, and make sure that you use a cutting mat to protect your work surface! Finally use your scissors to carefully cut out all the pieces of the model that you are working on.

Before you start to assemble the model spend some time folding all the crease lines to ensure that they are nice and crisp.

Use glue sparingly on one side of the joint only. After you have joined the pieces together make sure that they are lined up accurately, then pinch them together to seal the joint.

Take care at each stage. The more care and accuracy you use when you make these models the better they will work and the better they will look. Have fun!

Nodding Donkey

Move the donkey and the head nods, powered only by the
weight of a couple of coins.
See pages 31-34.

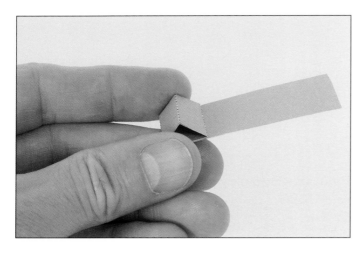

Step 1:
Mountain fold and glue together the
neck hanger.

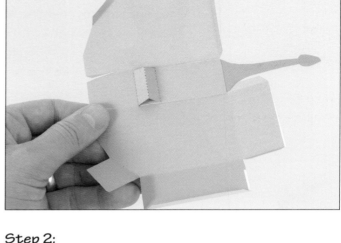

Step 2:
Glue the tail to the inside back of the body. Glue
the neck hanger to the inside top of the body,
lining it up with the back of the body.

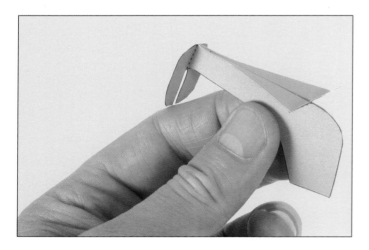

Step 3:
Glue the two halves of the neck together.

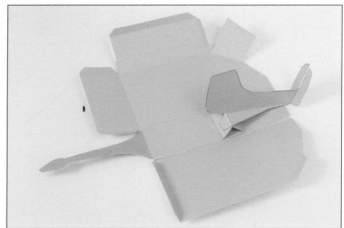

Step 4:
Glue the two tabs on the neck to the neck
hanger so that the neck hanger is free to swing
back and forth.

Step 5:
Wrap a coin in a strip of card. Make two of these.

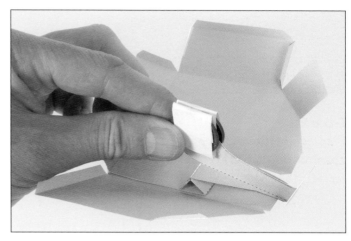

Step 6:
Glue the coins to the neck, one on each side.

Step 7:
Fold the body round and glue it together with the neck sticking out of the hole in the front and the tail sticking out the back.

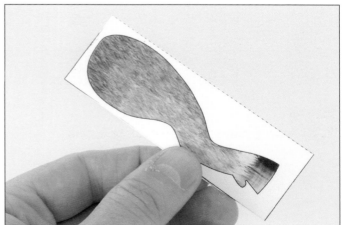

Step 8:
Score the leg pieces and mountain fold them. Glue the front to the back to double their thickness. Once the glue is dry, carefully cut them out.

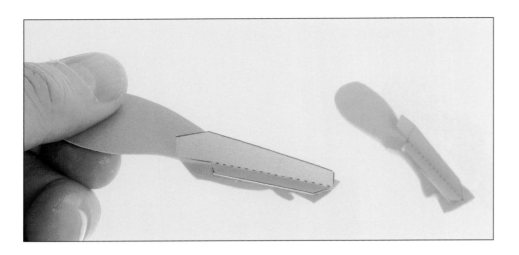

Step 9:
Once the glue is dry, carefully cut out the four legs. Glue a leg stiffener to the back of each leg.

Step 10:
Glue the four legs to the body.

Step 11:
Complete the model by adding the head to the neck. Once the glue is dry, tap the model or move it slightly to set it off nodding.

Flutter Box

A gift box to give to your true love!
Touch the box to make the heart flutter.
See pages 35-40.

Step 1:
Mountain fold and glue together the pivot.

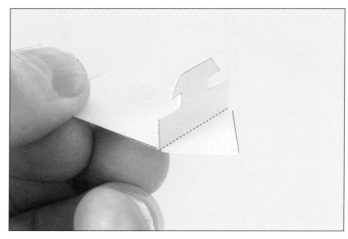

Step 2:
Once the glue is dry, carefully cut out the end.

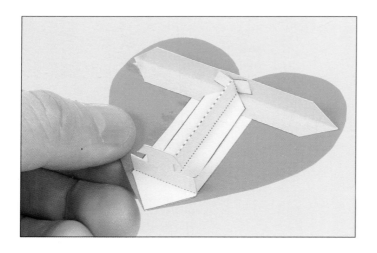

Step 3:
Glue the pivot to the back of the heart so that the point touches the tip of the heart. Glue the horizontal heart back to the back of the heart so that it touches the end of the pivot piece. Glue the vertical heart back between the two raised portions on the back of the heart.

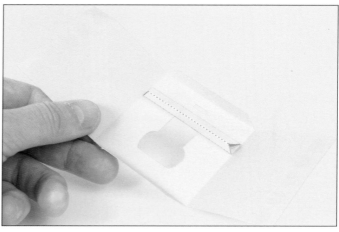

Step 4:
Fold up and glue together the box top stiffener. Glue the box top stiffener across the inside of the outer box piece so that the vertical edge touches the edge of the hole.

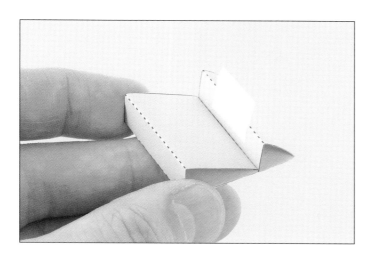

Step 5:
Fold round and glue together the pendulum. Glue the short hinge to the pendulum.

Step 6:
Glue the completed hanger to the box top stiffener.

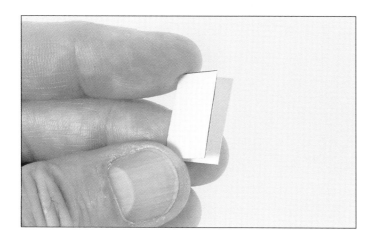

Step 7:
Fold the push rod in half.

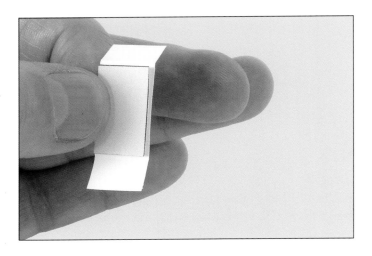

Step 8:
Glue the push rod around the long hinge.

Step 9:
Glue the completed push rod tab to the pendulum.

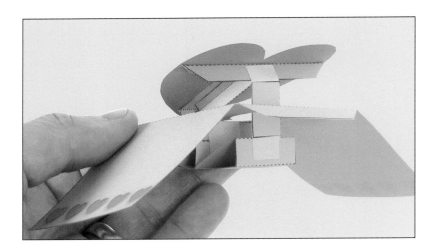

Step 10:
Fit the heart pivot into the slot in the box front. Glue the other end of the push rod tab to the heart top as shown.

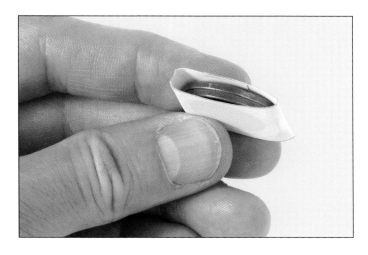

Step 11:
Fold two coins into the coin holder.

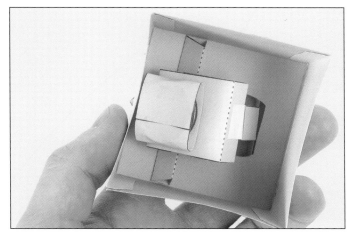

Step 12:
Glue the coin pack to the bottom of the pendulum.

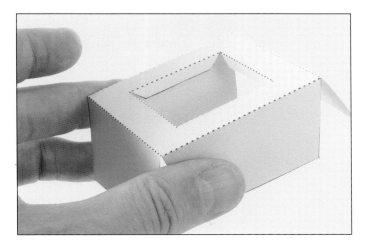

Step 13:
Mountain fold the inner box top.

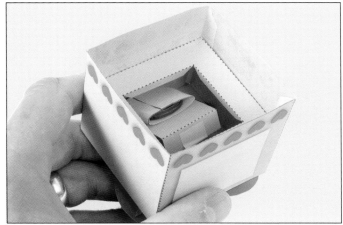

Step 14:
Attach the box sides to the outer box. Glue the inner box top into the outer box.

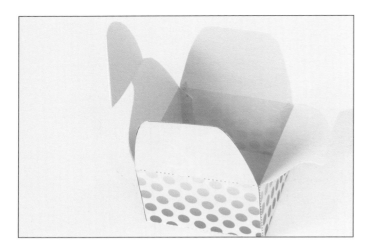

Step 15:
Assemble the lower box as shown.

Step 16:
Fill the lower box with chocolates for your true love.

Step 17:
Fold down the box top by slipping the two halves of the heart together. Slip the outer box over the lower box to complete the project.

Rockin' Robin

The robin will look cute sitting on your windowsill. Tap the box and watch him bob up and down just like the real thing!
See pages 41-44.

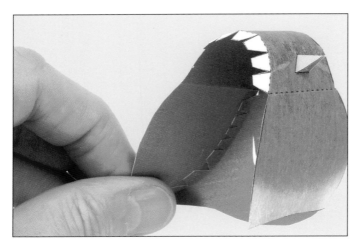

Step 1:
Cut out the body front and back and the two sides. Push the beak through the hole and attach it to the body from underneath. Attach one side to the body.

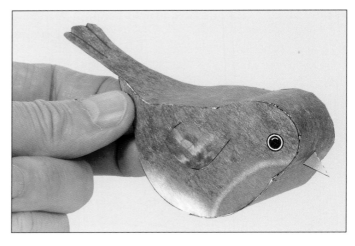

Step 2:
Glue the second side to the body. Be careful to keep the edges lined up.

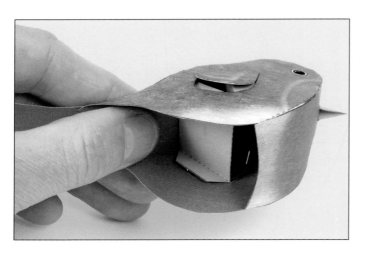

Step 3:
Glue the large leg support inside the body. Notice how it aligns with the wing hole in the picture.

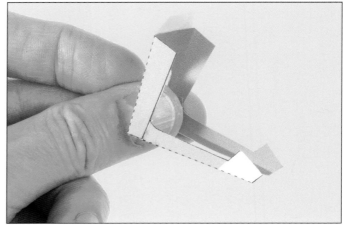

Step 4:
Fold up and glue together the legs.

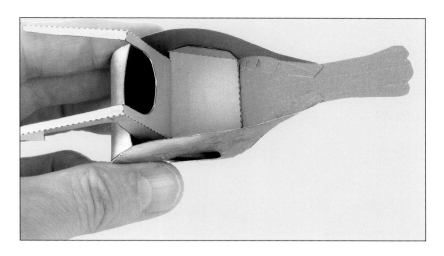

Step 5:
Glue the tab on the legs to the leg support.

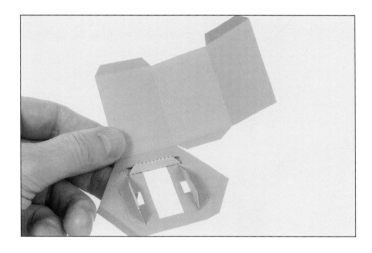

Step 6:
Fold up and glue together the box top stiffener to make a triangular tube. Glue it into place as shown. Glue the two small leg supports into place so that they just touch the edge of the leg holes in the box top.

Step 7:
Glue the box side into place, then glue on the box base.

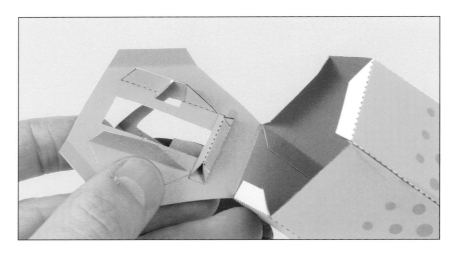

Step 8:
Thread the feet through the holes in the box top and glue them to the leg supports. Notice that the front of the box is the joint where the lid joins the box. Make sure that the robin faces to the front.

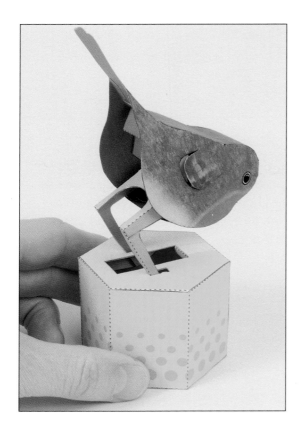

Step 10:
Fold and glue together the pendulum.

Step 9:
Fold the lid down and glue it into place.

Step 11:
Glue the hinge to the front of the pendulum, then glue the other end of the hinge to the gray area on the box top. Attach the wings.

Step 12:
Glue the push rod end inside the body. Connect the push rod between the pendulum end and the push rod end.

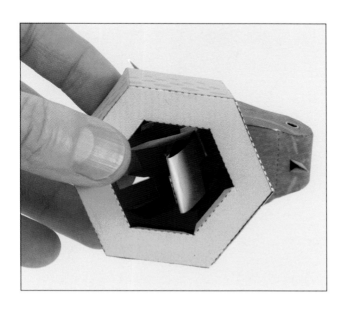

Step 13:
Wrap a two coins in a strip of card. Make two of these. Glue the two coin packs to the front and back of the pendulum to complete the model.

Rollin Bones

Set the bones on a downhill slope and watch
them jump and shake their way to the bottom!
See pages 45-46.

Step 1:
After scoring the dashed lines, mountain fold the four paper tubes toward the center and glue the ends of the tubes as shown. Be careful not to use too much glue!

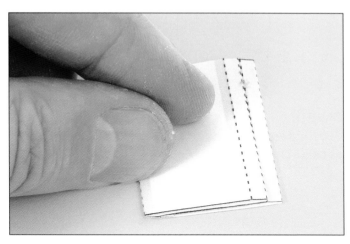

Step 2:
Fold one side of the tube over and glue together.

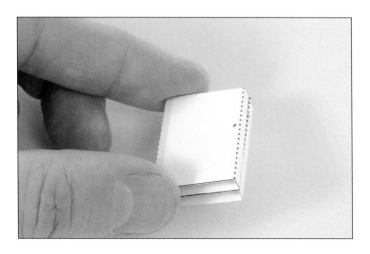

Step 3:
Construct the other tubes the same way. Glue two tubes together to make a bone. Make two bones.

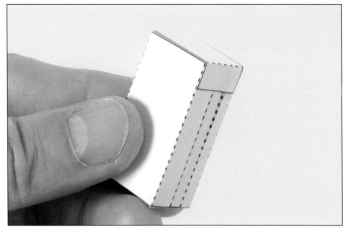

Step 4:
Glue an end cap onto one side of each bone.

Step 5:
Drop a penny into each of the four slots, then attach the other two end caps to the bones.

Step 6:
Score the side pieces and mountain fold them. Glue the front to the back to double the thickness. Once the glue is dry, carefully cut them out.

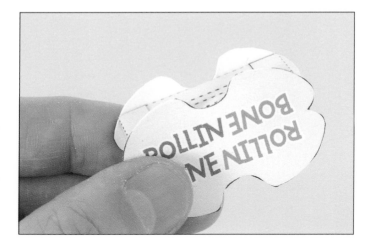

Step 7:
Turn the bones so the white side is facing up. Complete the project by gluing the side pieces into place on each bone.

Step 8:
Place the Rollin Bones on a slight slope and watch them go!

Tapping Feet

A pendulum powered paper project. Move the
box slightly and the foot taps impatiently.
See pages 47-52.

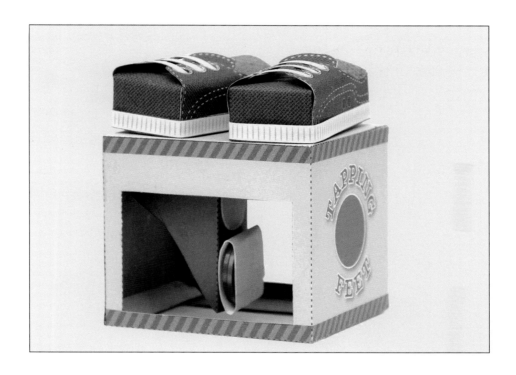

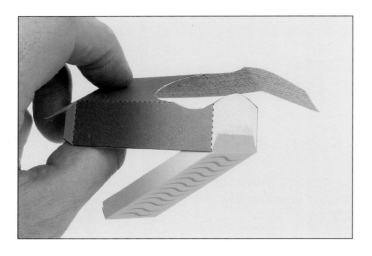

Step 1:
Starting with the left foot, glue the base of the shoe to the back of the foot.

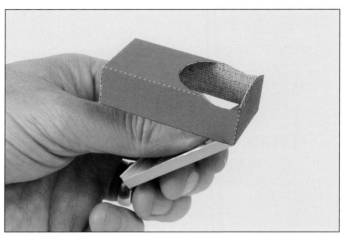

Step 2:
Glue the top of the shoe together.

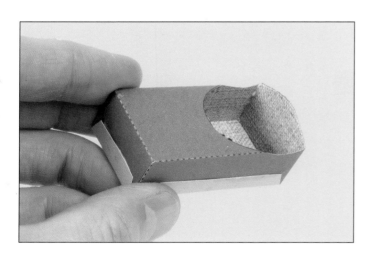

Step 3:
Glue the base to the outside of the shoe.

Step 4:
Align the flat edge of the tongue with the base of the shoe and glue it into place. Attach the sides of the shoe.

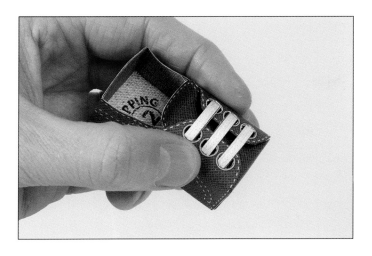

Step 5:
Curve the shoe sides over towards the middle of the shoe. Add a dot of glue to the end of each lace and glue them into place. Hold the shoe sides in position as the glue dries.

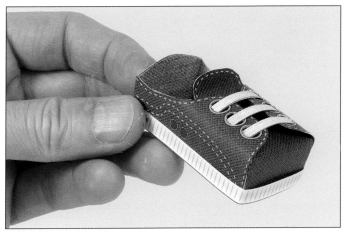

Step 6:
Starting with the side of the shoe at the back, wrap the rand around the bottom of the shoe and glue into place. The back portion of the shoe is plain.

Step 7:
Assemble the right shoe following steps 1 through 6. The only difference is that the base of the right shoe folds up halfway to allow room for a push rod.

Step 8:
Fold up and glue down the two triangular sections on the box.

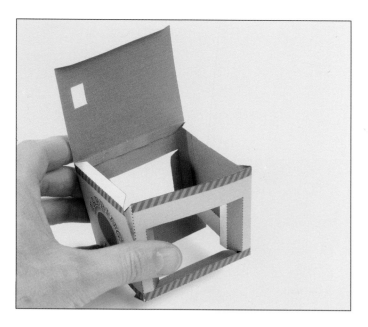

Step 9:
Glue the two halves of the box together and glue on the box top.

Step 10:
With the box top on a flat surface, glue the base flaps down, and then glue the side flaps down to the inside sides of the box. Assemble the pendulum hanger and glue it into place across the center of the box.

Step 11:
Glue together the pendulum and hinge.

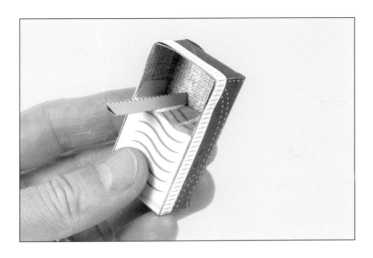

Step 12:
Fold up the triangular push rod and glue it to the foot in the position shown.

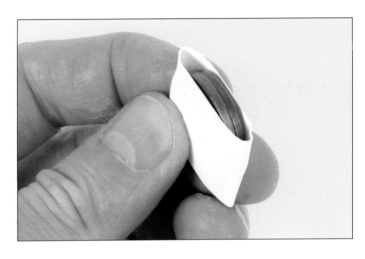

Step 13:
Fold up two coins in a wrap of paper.

Step 14:
Glue the coin pack to the pendulum. Glue the hinge on the back of the left foot so that the push rod fits nicely through the hole in the box top. Move the box, even slightly, and the foot taps impatiently.

Wag the Dog

Tap the box and the cute dog wags its tail!
See pages 53-58.

Step 1:
Mountain fold and glue the end of the box front to make a triangular tube.

Step 2:
Mountain fold and glue the end of the box back to make a smaller triangular tube.

Step 3:
Fold and glue the flaps on the box sides to make right angled triangle tubes.

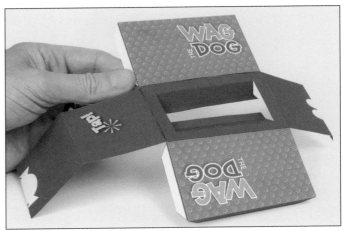

Step 4:
Glue the four sides to the base.

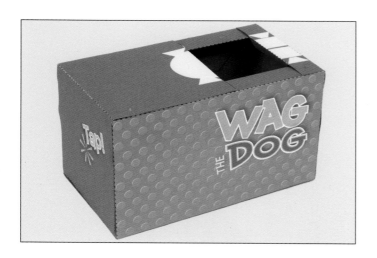

Step 5:
Fold the sides and glue them together to complete the box.

Step 6:
Fold and glue together the tail stand. Glue the tail hinge to the tail stand. Glue the tail platform to the hinge, lining it up along the length of the tail stand.

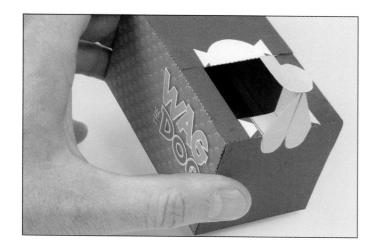

Step 7:
Glue the tail stand to the gray areas on the box.

Step 8:
Assemble the pendulum. Attach the
hinge and the push rod.

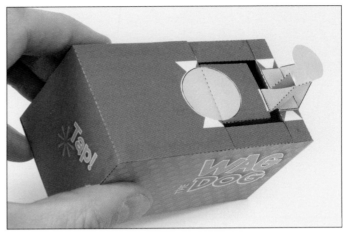

Step 9:
Fit the pendulum into the box. Glue the other
end of the push rod to the tail platform.

Step 10:
Gently curve the body round. Glue the
body to the gray areas on the box.

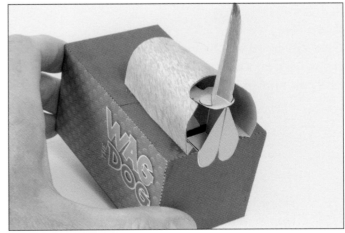

Step 11:
Glue the tail to the tail stand.

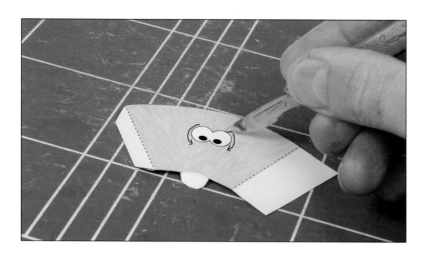

Step 12:
Cut down either side of the eyes with a craft knife. (Make sure an adult is present before using the craft knife!)

Step 13:
Glue together the head. Attach the nose and ears.

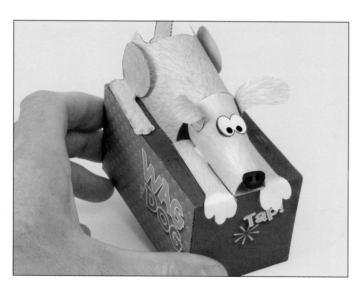

Step 14:
Glue the head to the box, then attach the front legs to the box. Glue the rear legs to the body as shown in the picture.

Step 15:
Make up two coin packs each with two coins. Glue the coin packs to the pendulum, front and back. Once the glue is dry, tap the box and the dog wags his tail!

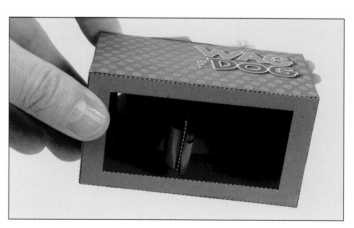

MODELS

Nodding Donkey

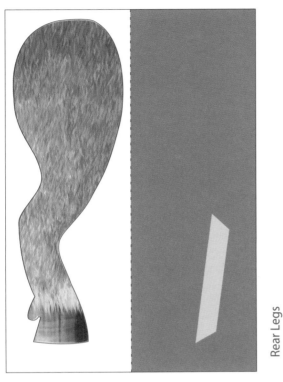

Rear Legs

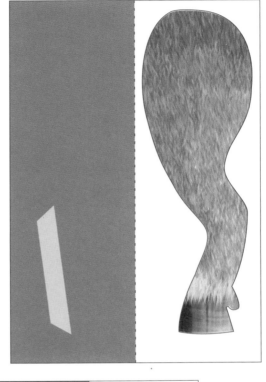

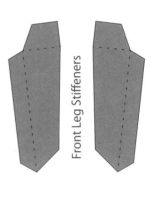

Front Leg Stiffeners

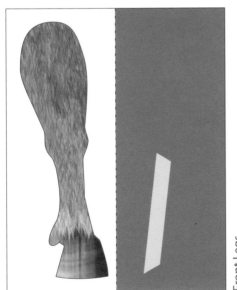

Front Legs

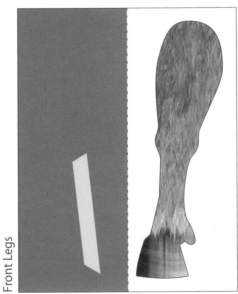

Rear Leg Stiffeners

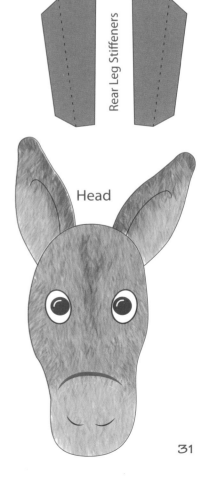

Head

Tail

31

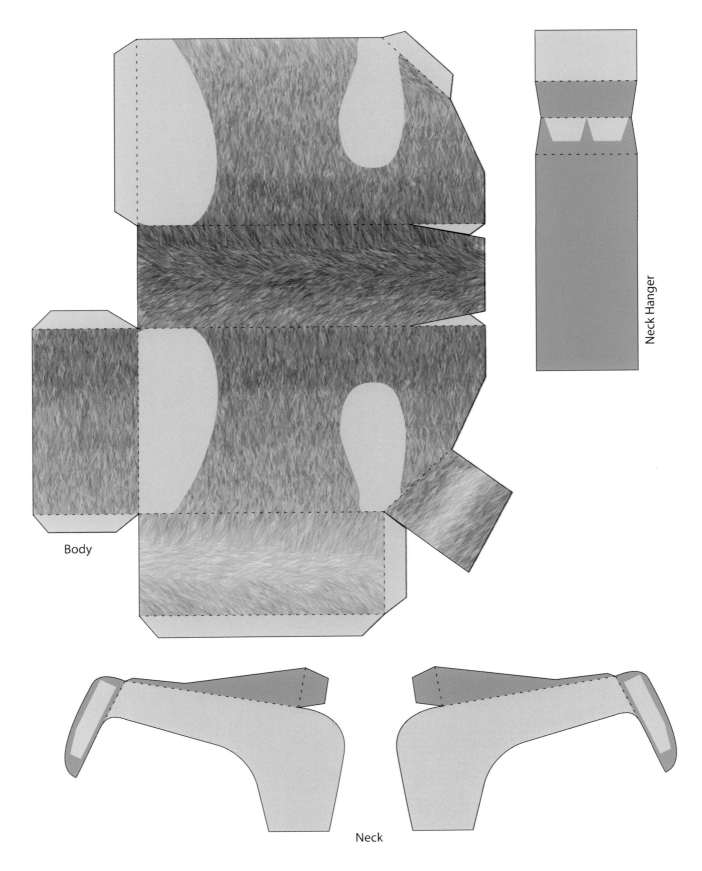

Body

Neck Hanger

Neck

34

Flutter Box

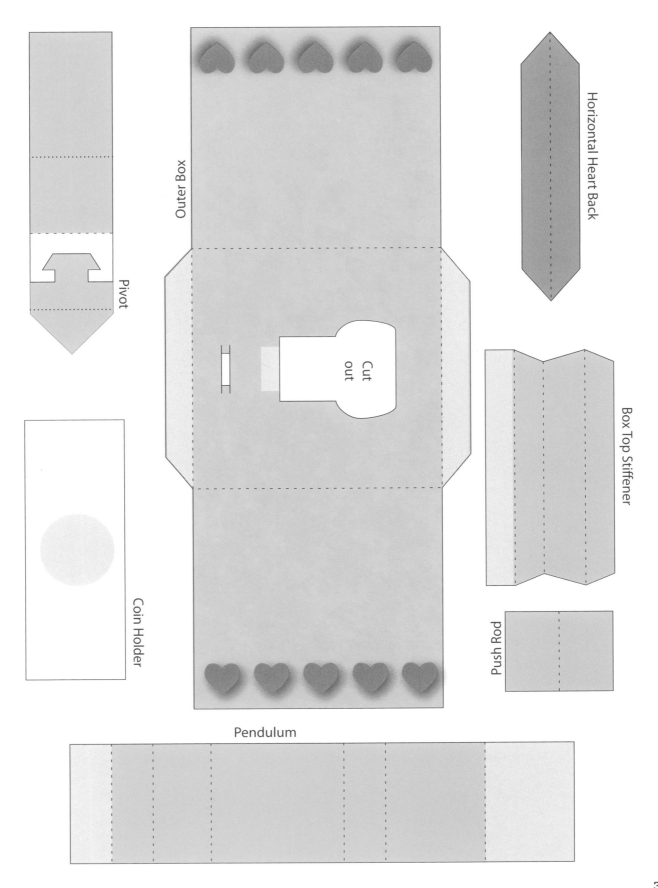

Outer Box

Horizontal Heart Back

Pivot

Cut out

Box Top Stiffener

Push Rod

Coin Holder

Pendulum

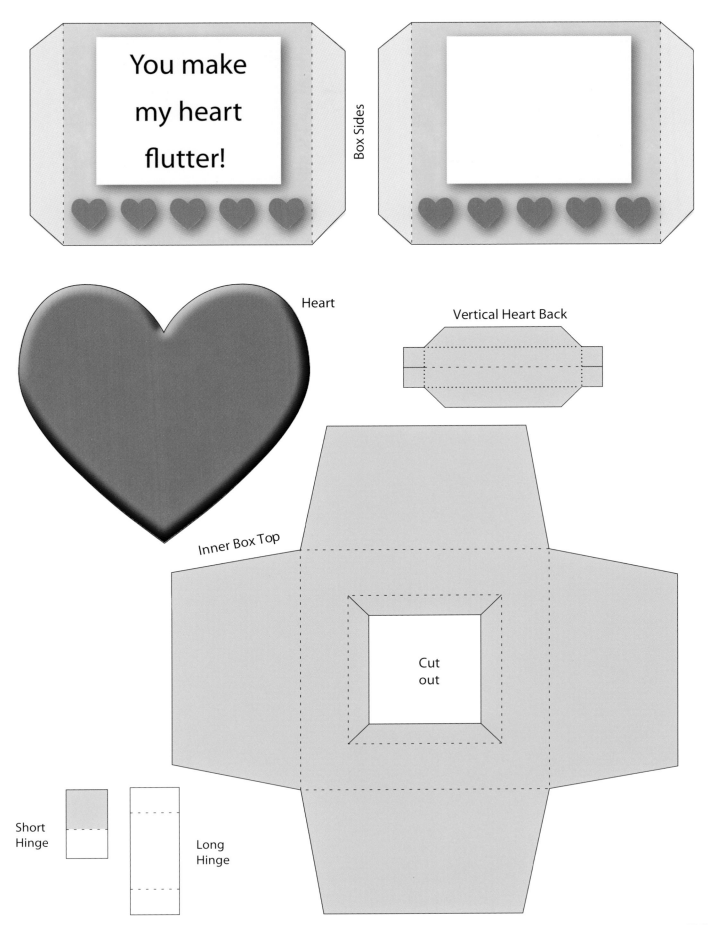

You make my heart flutter!

Box Sides

Heart

Vertical Heart Back

Inner Box Top

Cut out

Short Hinge

Long Hinge

37

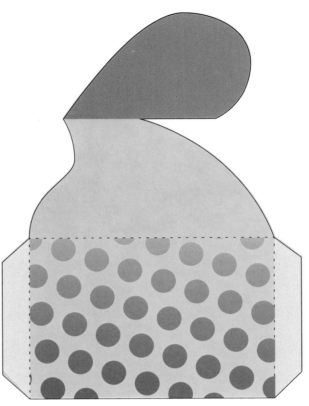

Lower Box Pieces

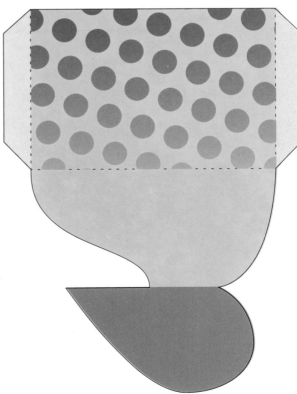

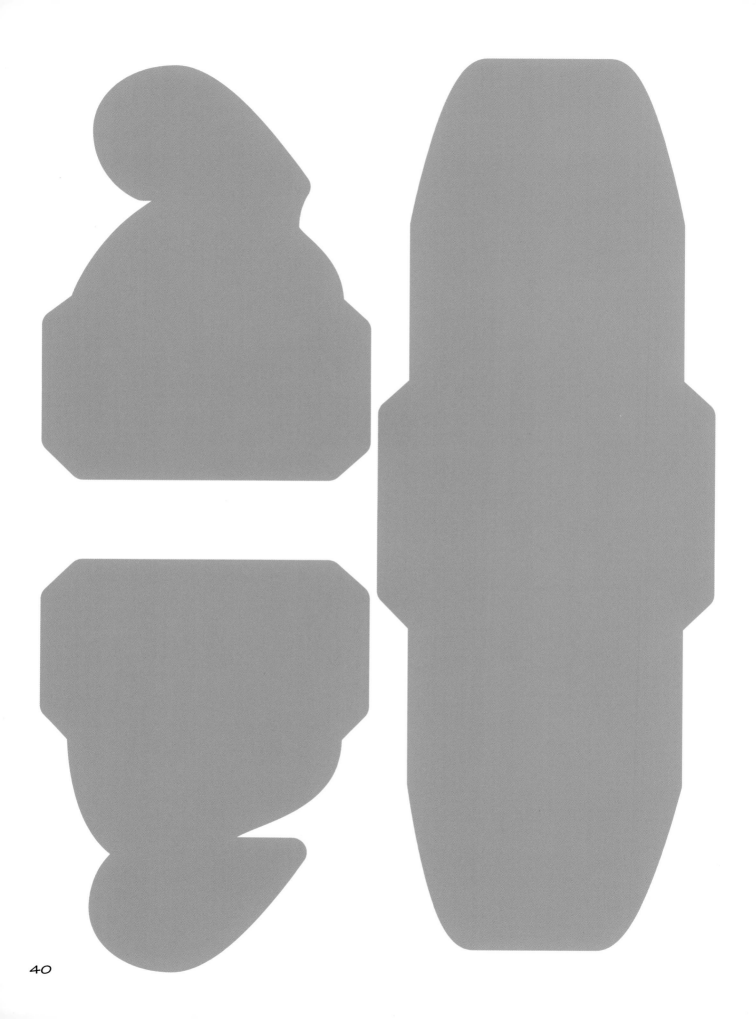

Rockin' Robin

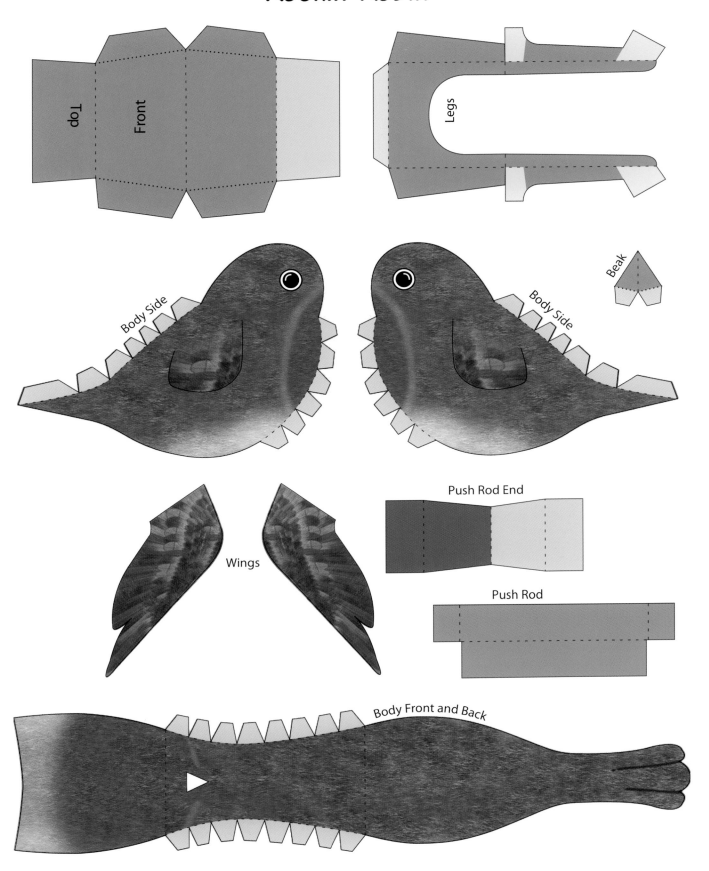

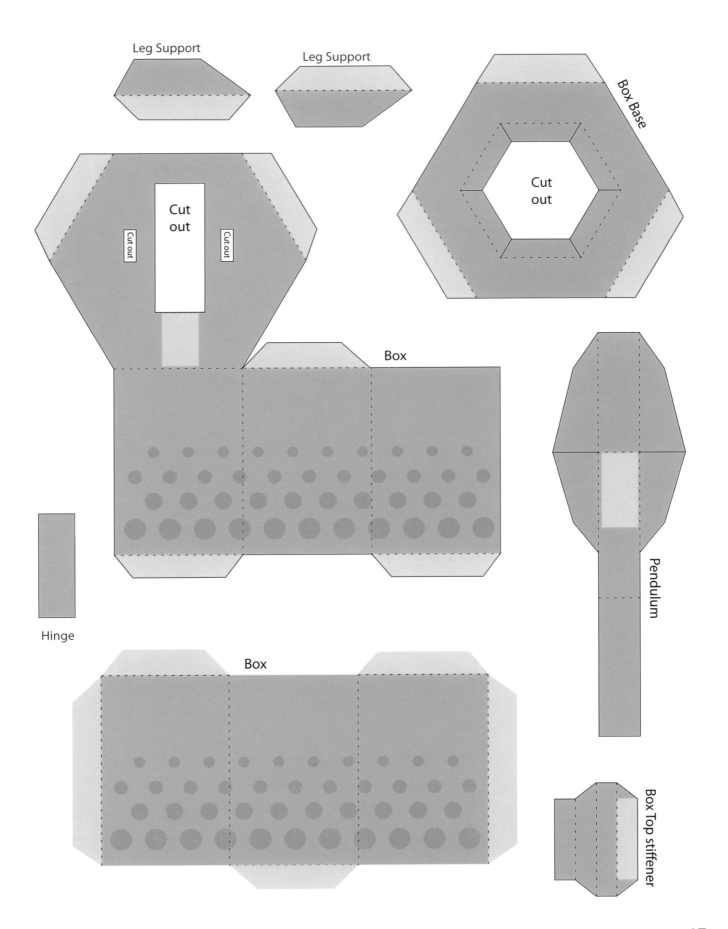

Leg Support

Leg Support

Box Base

Cut
out

Cut
out

Cut out

Cut out

Cut
out

Box

Pendulum

Hinge

Box

Box Top stiffener

Rollin Bones

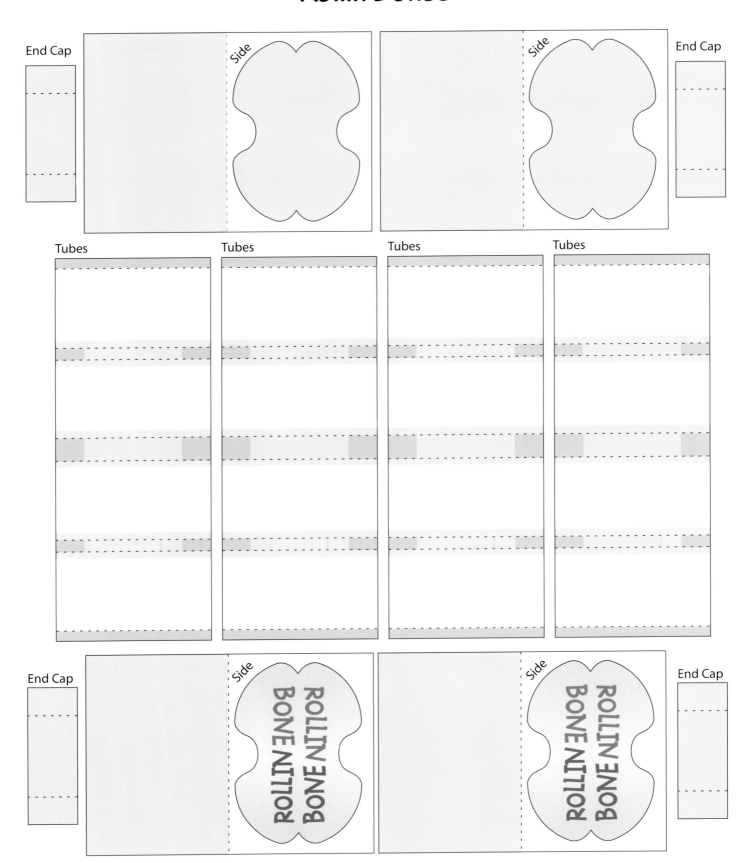

End Cap

Side

Side

End Cap

Tubes

Tubes

Tubes

Tubes

End Cap

Side

ROLLIN BONE
ROLLIN BONE

Side

ROLLIN BONE
ROLLIN BONE

End Cap

45

Tapping Feet

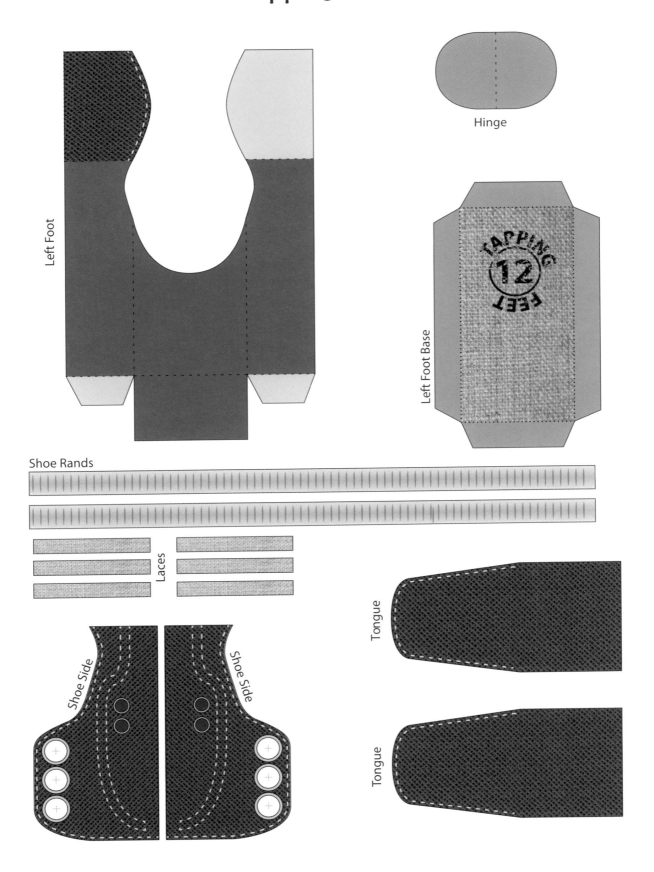

Left Foot

Hinge

Left Foot Base

TAPPING 12 FEET

Shoe Rands

Laces

Shoe Side

Shoe Side

Tongue

Tongue

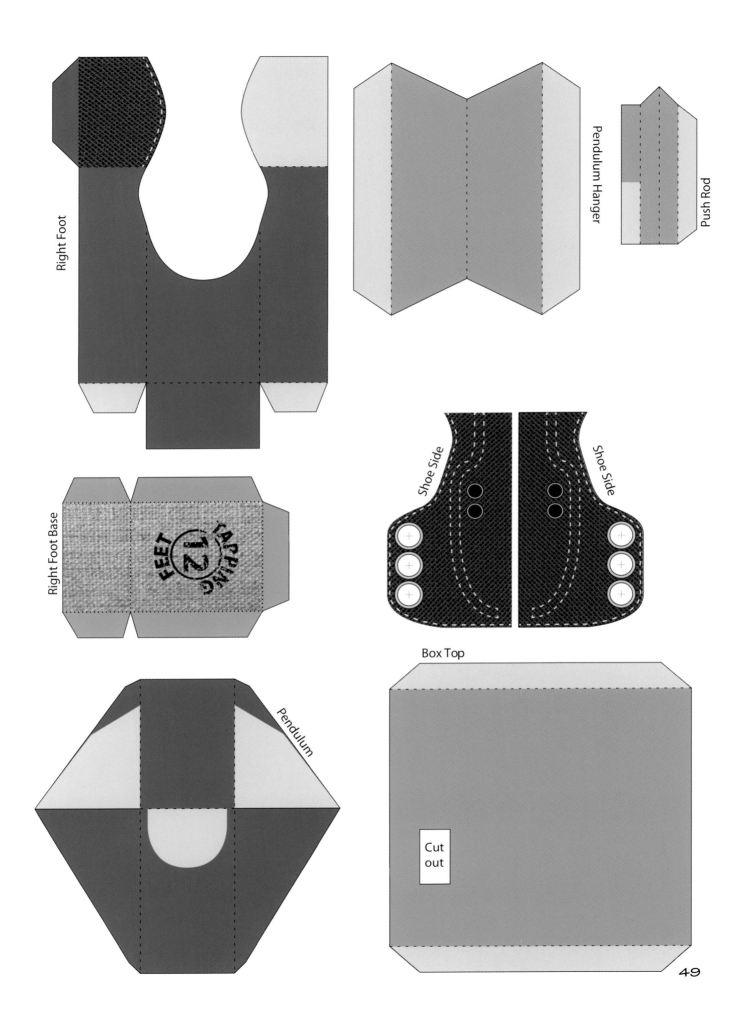

Right Foot

Right Foot Base

FEET TAPPING 12

Pendulum

Pendulum Hanger

Push Rod

Shoe Side

Shoe Side

Box Top

Cut out

49

Box

Cut
out

TAPPING
FEET

Box

Cut
out

TAPPING
FEET

51

Wag the Dog

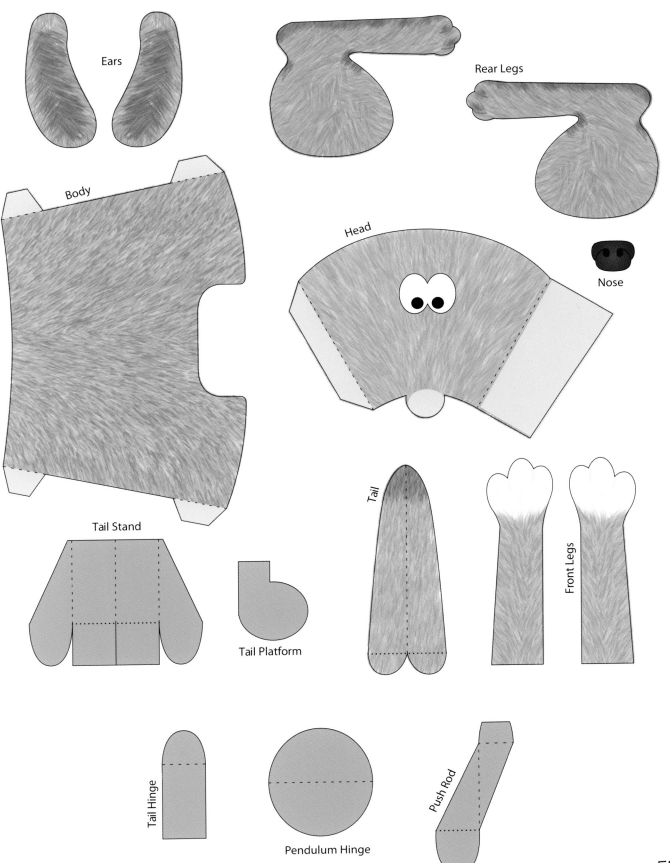

Ears

Rear Legs

Body

Head

Nose

Tail Stand

Tail Platform

Tail

Front Legs

Tail Hinge

Pendulum Hinge

Push Rod

54

Box Side

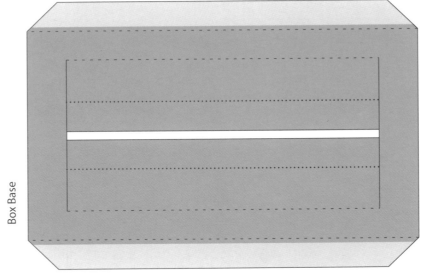

Box Base

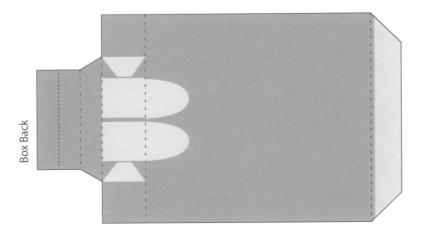

Box Back

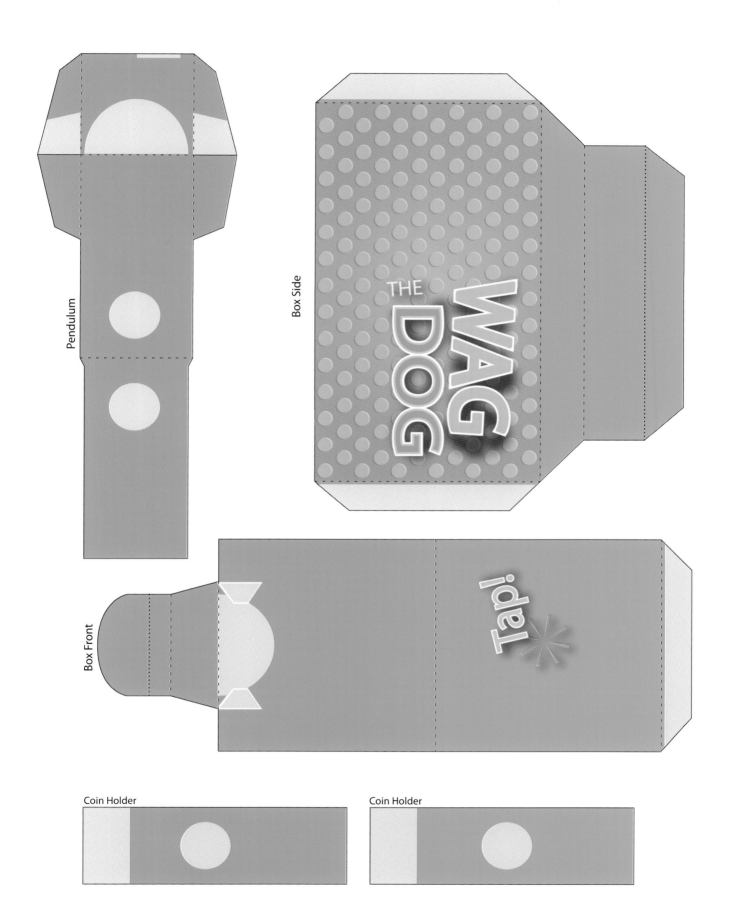

Pendulum

Box Side

THE
WAG
DOG

Box Front

Tap!

Coin Holder

Coin Holder

57

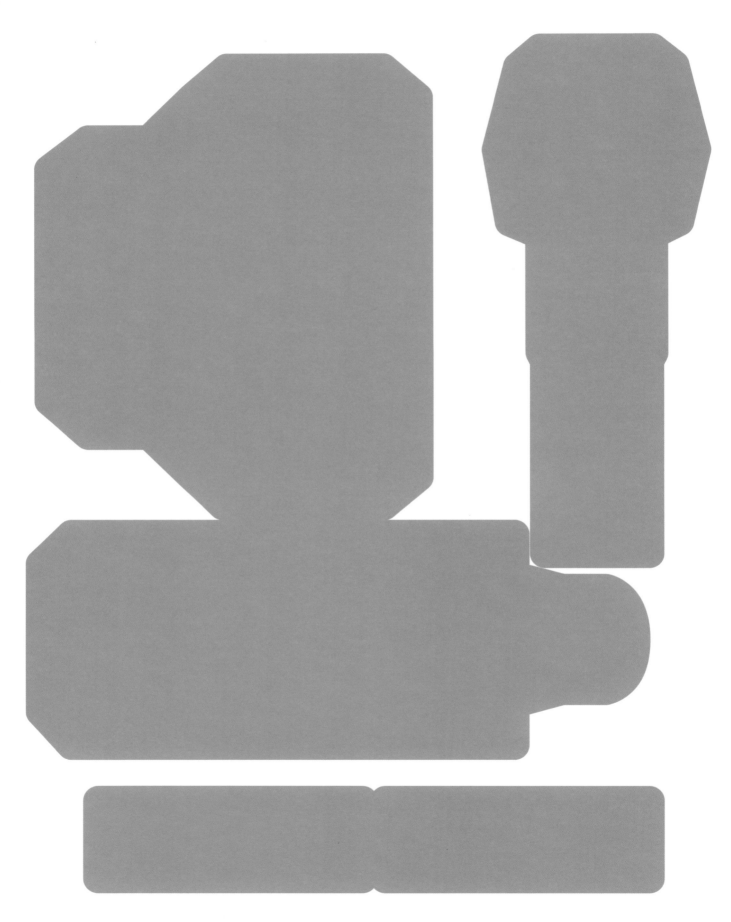